KITKITDIZZI

A NON-LINEAR MEMOIR
OF THE HIGH SIERRA

ANN & JOHN BRANTINGHAM

BAMBOO
DART
PRESS

LOS ANGELES † NEW YORK † LONDON † MELBOURNE

Kitkitdizzi by Ann and John Brantingham

978-1-947240-37-7 (Paperback)

978-1-947240-38-4 (eBook)

Cover art by Ann Brantingham

Layout and design by Mark Givens

Author photo by Alexis Rhone Fancher

For information:

Bamboo Dart Press

chapbooks@bamboodartpress.com

Bamboo Dart Press 028

www.pelekinesis.com

www.bamboodartpress.com

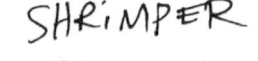
www.shrimperrecords.com

Dedicated to all of our High Sierra friends, but especially to Jenny, Jonathan, Tim, Scott, Carly, Denise, Colleen, Malinee, Erica, Savannah, Brian, Twyla, Jennifer, Kathy, Julie, Steve, Alpin, Katie, Gary, Maria, Stephh, Michael, Anne, and Sarah.

Some of these drawings have been previously published in *Cholla Needles Magazine*, *Crossing the High Sierra*, and *Words and Images*.

Some of these essays were previously published in *Worthing Flash, Come Shining: Essays and Poems on Writing in a Dark Time, The Los Angeles Review, Parks and Points*, and *Permanent Vacation II*.

Essays

ILLUSTRATIONS

FOREWORD

For the past ten years, my wife Ann and I have volunteered at Sequoia and Kings Canyon National Parks, and, for a while, I was the poet laureate of the parks. We have done trail trekking, invasive plant removal, camp hosting, and anything else we're capable of doing. Mostly what we have done is teach classes in poetry, prose, and art to volunteers who have come from all around the country to join us. This work is a collection of memoir snippets from that time. My memoir is told in words. Ann's is in images. This place and time has changed who we are and how we see the world.

KITKITDIZZI

Kitkitdizzi, pronounced "kit kid dizzy," is a low bush that grows in the sunnier parts of the High Sierra. It often is found on the sides of paths, and it has a lot of names. Most people know it as mountain misery. Other people know it as bear clover. Its scientific name is *Chamaebatia foliolosa*. I've always liked the original term, kitkitdizzi. I like the way it rolls about in my mouth.

If you take a leaf between your fingers and crush it, it emits a particular odor. About a third of the people who smell it like it. About a third are indifferent. About a third hate it. It's just body chemistry as to whether you enjoy its scent or not. It's like anything else in this world. Some people like cashews, coffee, video games, going to the movies, driving cars, flying in airplanes, or cooking gourmet meals. Other people don't. Some people like losing themselves in the backwoods and hope they are never found but are left to their silence. Others hate that silence.

I am one of the people who loves the smell of kitkitdizzi. When I walk by a bush, I brush an outstretched hand through it and inhale as deeply as I can.

Waking with Ghosts

I wake up in the bluing dawn with the ghost of Burnette G. Haskell bent over one side of my cot and the ghost of James J. Martin leaning over the other. It wasn't either of them who woke me, not when they came through the flap of my tent, nor when they stood silently in the clothing and facial hair straight out of the 1800s. I am up because of the light filtering through my white canvas walls and somewhere in my deep animal unconscious I know the sounds of early-morning birds and mammals even though I've lived in the city most of my life. The three of us stare at each other for a moment. Then I shift and blink, and they are gone.

I move as slowly and quietly as I can, but despite my best efforts, Annie stirs. She would have in a moment anyway. We are alive to the sounds of the mountains now, and she could no more sleep through them than she could through an alarm clock. Only, this isn't a single screaming noise terrifying her into a state of fearful consciousness. This is the world coming alive all at once, and for the summer, she and I are of this world, a part of it rather than visiting it. She is just another part of the biosphere awakening right here and now.

Haskell and Martin are part of it too. They were anyway, over a hundred years ago in this place that has become Sequoia and Kings Canyon National Park. I put the kettle on and watch them walk out of camp over the rise to the little meadow that I know is populated with bears this morning, at least a cinnamon bear and her two cubs. They've been waddling through every morning as I finish my tea, and I've had to chase them off every day for a week.

Annie and I conjured Haskell and Martin last night with our conversation. I've just finished reading about them. These were two of the men who formed the Kaweah Colony, a utopian community of socialists who came into the High Sierra before we had these national parks. They wanted to log the trees, and they found a kind of happiness away from the corrupting influences of city life.

So many of us have worked to find our separate peace. Haskell and Martin thought they could find utopia. They moved here and named the world's largest tree the Karl Marx Tree. It would later be the General Sherman Tree, the name it has kept until today. Of course, you cannot log these woods. The mind screams out against it, no matter how beautiful their dream. They were eventually driven out when President Benjamin Harrison protected the groves of giant sequoias.

He ordered the U.S. Army to guard the forests, and the Army sent the Buffalo Soldiers led by Colonel Charles Young. I hope they found peace here too for the summer months when they would be sent on patrol from San Francisco's Presidio. Colonel Young's ghost is wandering around here too. It's likely he's in the meadow with the cinnamon bear and her cubs driving out Haskell and Martin.

In a while, Annie and I sip our tea and let the morning into our bodies. We don't need coffee. We don't need to think. We don't need to know what the news is, and we don't care what the traffic will be like. There's no point even in learning the weather forecast. It will be what it will be.

After a while, I point off in the direction where Haskell and Martin might be. "Do you want to go take a look at the meadow?"

I ask, but I don't tell her why I really want to go. I'd like to see Colonel Young on his horse in full uniform driving them out of a forest that lives permanently in the 1890s.

"Sure," Annie says. "Shirley is probably up and eating breakfast." Shirley is what we've named the cinnamon bear. We trudge uphill as quietly as we can, hoping not to break the world the morning has established. We cross the road and jog up the little embankment on the other side, walking until we get to a high spot that looks down on a little meadow that only she and I go to. We're the only people, anyway. We can take it all in here, and although I can see the bear we named Shirley tearing open a log with her long claws to get at the termites, I cannot see Colonel Young or Haskell or Martin.

I suppose they're off someplace else, dreaming the thoughts of the dead. Maybe they're just tired of me. Maybe the sun is too high now for the early morning visions and visitations, but Annie pulls on my arm and points across to the other side of the field.

"Look," she says.

It takes me a moment to focus, but soon I see a kid, maybe fifteen years old, sitting in the shade on a boulder. He's trying to be still so the bear isn't spooked. He has dark brown hair, and he's curled into himself, hugging his knees to his chest and content to watch silently. "That's me," I say, and I am right.

I am a ghost here too, the ghost of the child I once was. I spent many of my summers wandering these trails, watching bears and deer and wondering where my place in this world was. I came here chased by nuclear dread and depression and the terror of growing into adulthood, and my childhood self still lives here. He wanders through the woods, dreaming the silent long thoughts of his youth. My breath catches to see him because he is such a rare sighting any more, and this might be the last time in my life that I ever get a glimpse of him. I want him to see me too. I want to look into his eyes to see what he thinks of me, if I am a failure to him. If he admires who I have become.

Except, I watch him silently as his eyes follow the bear. I am afraid that if I move, he will notice me. I'm terrified that if I make a noise, he will bolt, and when I look the other way for a moment, he slips away.

MOTH NOCTURNE

The two great losses of my early childhood move from Pennsylvania to California were the fireflies of summer and sledding in winter. They were my first connections to the natural world, learning how to live on the earth and be of the earth.

It wasn't until my parents took us to the High Sierra on a camping trip that I felt anything like that. Being a feral child, I'd slip away when everyone else slept, and one night I shrugged out of the sleeping bag to see the night in moonlight. There was a mercury light next to the bathroom, and in the light the moths were out and dancing.

I was too young to see anything but magic, and I caught one in the little cage I made of my fingers, and I inspected it up close. It was gray and fuzzy, and I remembered the fireflies I'd lost. These moths were maybe more precious because they didn't announce their presence. I had to hunt them out.

That the High Sierra is a place for moths is not surprising. Most places are, but we don't see them. They are animals of the night, and we prefer day. If you walk in the dark with a flashlight on or better if you sit outside with a light on, they'll be attracted to you, but I've always preferred to be in darkness at night.

A flashlight illuminates part of the nighttime world, but it makes all the rest invisible. As long as there is no cloud cover and the forest is not too dense, I always walk with one in my pocket or in my hand, but off. The stars are enough to navigate by, and if the moon is out I can see nearly as well by night as by day.

When I'm walking at night, I know there are moths only when

they brush my skin, sometimes on my cheeks. There is that moment of surprise, but not fear, not danger.

When you walk alone through the High Sierra at night without a flashlight or direction, just following your feet, you are no longer yourself.

Those who walk at night lose their identity. They are not their names or jobs or anything they have done. There is no before or after. They are just creatures wandering the woods.

It is such a relief to stop being me for a while. In those moments, I re-see the world for what it is or at least what it is for me. In a meadow, I do nothing but watch the grass stalks bending back and forth in the breeze. In the forest where the fir trees gather together to create deep shadows, I grope from one trunk to the next heading straight toward the place where the trees open up, and there is a splash of moonlight on the ground. I truly hear the wind.

The moths I see are precious, but so are those that are invisible to me. In the foothills, the yucca moths are dependent on their hosts, and their hosts need their moths. One provides food, and the other pollination. The moths are the same color as the stalks.

I have lived near yucca my whole life, and I've never seen a yucca moth. I've never searched for one either. Let them be. They are themselves, and I do not need to bother them.

I have seen moths dancing in shafts of moonlight cutting through the forest.

Sometimes at night, I visit bathrooms that have mercury lights and moths flitting about them. From a distance, I'd still grab a moth and look at him in the cage of my fingers, careful not to hurt the little animal. Once I reenter the light though I'm back to being myself, and I'm too inhibited to play with the animals, too sure that someone might see me and laugh. When you carry your identity with you, you feel it's important that no one should ever laugh in the wrong way.

When I think back to Pennsylvania, there were no moths in my world. I was distracted by the glamour of the firefly as most children are, and it makes me wonder what I missed there.

It makes me wonder what I am missing here, and there is a deliciousness to knowing that I do not know what is around me. The world is still as mysterious as religion. The identities that I carry with me are meant to eliminate the mystery. My labels tell me what I am allowed to see.

In the dark, my true self comes out, the feral child who crawled out into the night. He is ready to explore and sniff and move through the dark places. He does not fear laughter. He does not fear moths. He simply feels his way through the world.

Naming is the first act of love.

I can feel that love all over the forest, people who had insights, and saw things that other people didn't see. I love the etymology of a forest because that love seeps through the years, and you see the world as others see it.

From the valley as you look up into the mountain from the town of Lemon Grove, you can see the giant rock formation called Homer's Nose, named not for the ancient bard but for someone's dog. It does look from this distance like a dog's snout, falling off at the end, and I think of that person delighting in his dog's personality, finding a way to memorialize their friendship.

I love the name Moro Rock, a word given to it by the Native Americans, and we're not sure what it means, but on the coast three hundred miles from here is another rock in the same formation sitting in the surf. Its name is Morro Rock, and I imagine the commerce between those two places, the surprise someone must have had seeing how the two different places had the one same feature.

I love the names Hospital Rock, Sunset Rock, the Giant Forest, and Halstead Meadow although I don't know who Halstead was. Perhaps he named the place after himself in a moment of self-definition. If he did, he was loved well enough that the term stuck.

I love the tree named after Colonel Charles Young, the buffalo soldier who was the park's first superintendent. They tried to name it for him while he was alive, but he didn't have the ego for it. He asked them to name it after a real hero, Booker T. Washington. His men waited until he had died and then named another tree after him so he would have the monument he deserved.

I love the names of the plants. Kitkitdizzi, of course. Maybe my favorite name is after a well-known botanist. Bigelow's sneezeweed is named for him. There are many plants in these forests named for Bigelow, but I imagine the moment that led up to that designation. A man named Munz came through the chaparral areas of the mountains and found an iris that grows only in the Marble Fork of the Kaweah River. This is named Munz's Iris. It is a treasure that almost no one gets to see, and he loved it and named it after himself.

There is Muir Rock named for the Scot who wrote about this area. He described it accurately, but at first no one could believe that what he was writing could possibly be true. He stood on that rock and lectured about the need to preserve the wild places of the West and along with Steven Mather, Roosevelt and a number of other people came up with a plan that became the national parks system. Those who lived here loved him and named that place for him. There is a millipede on the other side of the park that lives only in one cave in the world. It is named for him too.

All of this lies along the Great Western Divide, which is a grand thing and a grand name, but I think I prefer terms like kitkitdizzi and the Muir millipede. I like to think of people finding small things that are personal and pouring their love into them. I like to think about how that love changed them. I like to see the world through their eyes.

RUNNING WITH THE BEAR

In the morning, I hike up to Heather Lake alone, taking nothing but the clothes I'm wearing. It's sunny and warm so I wear a tee shirt, shorts and running shoes. It's a long uphill climb, but the day cools by degrees, and by the time I hike the four miles, it's clouded over too. The view is beautiful. On one side Alta Peak rises out of the treeline and is snowcapped. On the other, I look down past Tokopah Falls to the canyon where the Marble Fork of the Kaweah River rushes toward Lodgepole.

I walk back to camp in a different direction than I came, cresting a mountain. Just as I am on the broad and flat ridgeline, the clouds darken up, and it starts to rain. I speed up my trudge, which is made easier by the fact that I'm going downhill. Soon, the rain gets harder, and in ten minutes it's hailing, the little stones stinging my skin, but they don't really hurt, and the day is so cool, I start to jog downhill. In a moment, the lightning starts, but it's not directly on top of me.

I've never had a moment like this before, running through a lightning and hail storm, the thunder like something out of a Wagnerian opera. I'm going down the ridgeline which is perhaps only twenty yards wide, so when a black bear sees me charging, he assumes there is something to run from and starts his own gallup downhill, running in a kind of easy lope. For a moment, maybe five seconds, we're running together, me on the trail, him through the trees, but together.

I will try to explain the sensation of running with a bear through the lightning and hail when I get back, but it falls flat with everyone I tell.

We leave in the early morning just before dawn while the light is still bluing. The first colors we can see are the greens of the pine needles, but everything else is muted, still gray on the ground. There are ten of us in the class. Some of us students, some teachers. Some of us are young, eighteen or nineteen, and we have never seen the forest before. Everything is new and surprising. Some of us have been hiking for sixty years, and we are still strong enough outside and in to keep going. Most of us are in between those two ages.

We hike upward. The truth of most High Sierra hiking is that we go upward on the way out, and a kind of hopeless fatigue washes over us as we realize that this pushing is our lot in life for the next few hours. That hopelessness is forgotten soon enough, replaced by memories of the first time we hiked this way with our mother, the way she crouched down and pointed out how a beetle can be beautiful if we watch it without eyes of fear. We had screeched at it when we were home and a beetle walked across the kitchen floor. That day she had picked it up calmly and thrown it out the window. We think about her now.

We think about that trip we took the week before we were to ship out to the Vietnam War. Back then we thought that maybe the memory of this place would help a little. And it did. Not much, but a little.

We think of our college classes waiting for us when we get back. We think of Mikey, who promised to marry us and now has just disappeared. We wonder where he has gone, if it was something that we did, if we could say the right thing to make him come back, to make him love us again.

Up at the first stream crossing, we have to stop. "What is it?" one of us asks.

"Wildflowers." And it is true, a field of them so thick we cannot see the stream for the plants, and we think about our friends. Back home, we are known as the tough one on the team. Would they all laugh now if they saw us gazing at a field of flowers? On the other hand, what does that matter? The only thing that matters is right here and now, and these people get it. They really get it, and they're not going to laugh at us. They don't even seem to notice that we feel like crying a little bit. Actually crying. Hell, all the men have stopped with us and are watching the flowers waving in the early morning breeze.

We pause for a moment on the banks of that stream to get pictures, to sketch, and we crouch down at the bank and see that beetle, the same one from fifty years ago we saw when we were a little girl. We can feel our mother's hand on our back and hear her words. Her voice was different than everyone else's as though it understood us in a way no one else did and loved us for that understanding. It got into us and was still there wandering around inside us. It took this beetle to pull her back out.

When we finally get going again, we wander up to the front of the line. We are only eighteen years old, we've never seen a forest until this week, and everyone told us we were stupid to come up. They told us that we'd get eaten by a bear or lost, but the moment we got here, we knew none of that would happen. This place was more home than any place that has ever been, and now because we can, we hike more quickly than everyone else, speeding up the path ahead until we cannot even hear their voices any longer. As we come around the corner, there is a bear, one with a ginger colored head and a black body. It pauses a moment to stare at us. This is the moment we were warned about, the moment that terrorized us when we were down the mountain, and at this moment, the bear glances at us and goes back to sniffing out food. We stand here staring at it without fear, just lost in this moment where we understand that once we enter the forest, we are the forest just as the trees and the bears are. We stay there until the bear runs off when it hears the voices from the rest of the group. When they catch up, we do not tell them about the bear. The bear is our own personal memory that we will keep hidden in ourselves.

We push up the side of the mountain, a little faster than is comfortable. It's hard for us at nearly eighty years old to move, but there is joy in being able to do it. Anyway, we like what happens when we push our bodies. The energy, the young woman who used to live inside this body, who was always so fearless, is back. This is the woman who was unafraid to raise two children on her own, who saw it as a challenge to have those endless jobs. This is the way we remember her.

It is hard coming up these long hills, but out of breath, with the others talking about whatever it is they are going to talk about, we remember hot days in Vietnam. Mostly what we remember today is Tony, our best friend who was killed in the Tet offensive, but we don't think about that part of his story. Not today. Leave the dying for later. Today, what we remember is his laughter. We remember his joy. We think about those long stories Tony would tell that would lead off into nothing, and how he'd forget what he'd been saying, and by the end, it was a different story altogether and how everyone laughed at him for that, and loved him for it too.

It takes a while, but we get up to the cliffs along the Watchtower, with their thousand foot drop off, and we all pause a while to take pictures of ourselves smiling over the gaping chasm. We're terrified of this bit. We hate heights, and getting close to them, the breath is taken out of our lungs. Still, we are a part of this group, and we don't want to ruin it for everyone else, so we keep quiet and keep our eyes on the trail before us. That helps a little, but soon we start to hike again, and every once in a while, our eyes take control and peek over the edge, down those thousand feet. This, we realize, is the most terrifying thing conceivable, but we realize, we are doing it. There is nothing we can't do, we realize. We realize that we are stronger even than the fears that bury themselves inside of us. We are stronger than anything we might imagine, and fear is just that thing standing between us and joy.

It is wonderful for us to lean over the cliff. The boys at home will never believe that we did this so we take pictures of it. Maybe we won't talk about the bear, but we will tell everyone about that feeling of flight we got up on the cliff. Our sister will ask us if we were scared, and we'll scoff, and say there's nothing to be scared of. We'll want to prove that to her, to show her what this place is like, so we'll save money and vacation time for a month and take her. She'll love it too.

When finally we get to the lake, we'll realize this is our time alone. We'll take out that sketchbook and draw the reeds on the shore of the lake. We love the way they move, and while everyone else is exclaiming over the lake and the view of the waterfall below us and Alta Peak above us, we will understand that the grasses have as much beauty here as anything else. It is not just the big things of this world that matter and change us. Those tiny things do so as well. One of women of the group seems to be watching a bug crawling along the lakeshore, and we'll understand that she gets it too. This is maybe a truth the two of us could share, but there are other truths up here too that the others are understanding.

We have lunch on the shore of the lake and talk about trips. We talk about our favorite adventures. Some of us have been to Asia or South America. We have seen Europe and some of us have never been out of Los Angeles. We all agree that we love this lake though. We like to take off our boots and cool our feet in the glacial run off.

We go back a different way, over the ridge of the mountain away from the cliff. After we crest the mountain, some of the younger people start to run downhill, and the elk that lives inside of us is somehow awakened. We're only forty-three after all, and we start to run after them bouncing down the side of the mountain on the path in a way we used to when we remembered joy. We call to each other, whoop, forgetting that there may be pain, there probably will be pain, but there is hope, too. There is running downhill in the sunlight. This is the everything of now.

As some of us run down ahead, we start to talk about Tony, and it's like he's back. We tell about his family and how much he loved his girlfriend. We don't tell the rest of the story though, how we came back and met her and married her. We don't talk about how our wife never stopped loving him and how we never did either. This is Tony's story, not ours. We talk about what a good person he was.

We lie down and wait for the rest of the group to catch up and think about Mikey. This is the first time in a while that we haven't both hated him and wanted him back at the same time. This is the first time we realize that we don't actually want him back at all. Somehow, here on this boulder, we think that maybe he was right. He just wanted different things, and he was too young to settle down and maybe we are too. It's easy to be forgiving here. It's easy to remember to love him. He deserves it, after all. Everyone deserves love.

By the time we get back to the trailhead, we are all tired into silence. Someone says something about dinner and another one of us says he'll never have the strength to cook. That might be true, but that's all right. Once the fire gets started back at camp, those of us with enough energy to cook will cook. Those of us who can't will tell stories. We'll all laugh. We'll think about anything except for this hike up to Heather Lake and laugh until all that is left is that musical sound in the tree above our heads.

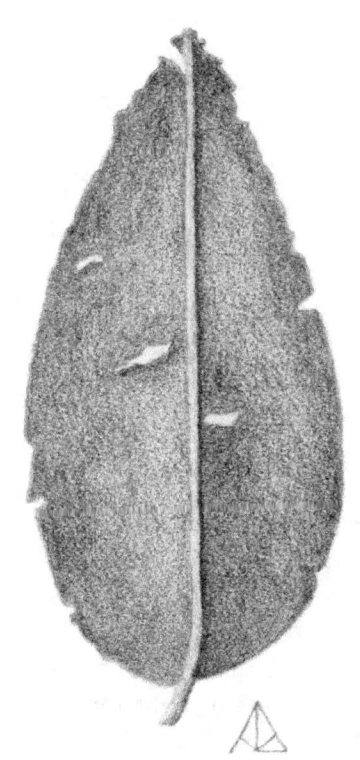

Walking through Bats

I come into our camp as the darkness is falling to see the camp-fire going with that quality of orange that firelight has on tree trunks when there is still a little blue left in the sky and you can still see between the trees, but it's a little hard. My friends gather chairs or cook food, chat, clean, and prepare themselves against the coming darkness. They are busy enough with the necessary chores that for the moment, they do not hear what I do, the near silent, squeaking conversation of bats who have come out for the evening.

The bats of course flit above us and around us. The bats dance near the fire and above my friends who have attracted mosqui-toes. The mosquitoes are attracted to me too, so the bats dance around me.

I can see the bats in their dance in the fire light above my friends, swooping in and out, but it's nearly impossible to watch them when they're near me. I can hear them squeak. They speak to me. They remind me of the past.

My mother introduced me to the bats when I was a child, and we walked around a meadow at night. I thought they were birds because for me bats didn't seem like real things. They were the stuff of cartoons and vampires. Watching them circling around, chasing after a meal, they didn't seem sinister. They weren't frightening in the ways that I imagined.

I sat on a boulder on the edge of the meadow and watched them in the last moments of light forgetting that it would be dark soon and that we weren't carrying a flashlight. When their show ended, I stood up to see we didn't need one. I could move through the forest by moonlight, and it felt safe and easy knowing that the bats had gone back to sleep in their trees or caves for the evening.

They remind me of my journeys underground, searching caves and mine shafts. When I was young enough to be immortal, I would seek these places out in the desert and climb down inside them. One time in the Saline Valley, a few feet inside, I looked up to see a clump of what seemed to be a hundred or more clinging to the ceiling and sleeping. There were a couple of guardians awake and flying about, but most of them huddled together hanging upside down and swaying together in a rhythm they understood. It was as though they'd been caught in a breeze, but there was no wind. They were pulsing together in the cool of the mineshaft despite the hundred degree weather outside.

When I saw them again that twilight, I thought of Mom and how she taught me that they were kind. It was like seeing friends and I waved to them. I could hear them squeaking around me telling me the secrets that bats know, and I do not.

This night, remembering that evening in the forest, I decide to watch the pageantry of the bats, the whole show. I imagine the microdecisions of those creatures. How in the moment they must be, how unconcerned with geopolitics. I think of Mom in her home now in the city. I wonder if she misses the bats.

They were there for me in the Lake District in England too when my wife and I wandered through the evening. It stays light for so long in summer there, but when the darkness finally came, I could hear them searching around on the same journey as their American cousins. We were leading a group of students from Los

Angeles, and while the country was foreign to them, the country-side was perhaps more so.

That morning I'd taught one of my students how to skip stones. She'd never heard of that before. Another one saw a sheep for the first time. There was water everywhere, creeks, rivers, lakes, things that people in Southern California don't see. If that was magic during the day, the twilight bats made the evening more so. We talked to them about how much these bats fed, what good they were doing for us, and we stayed outside until the moon lit our world. I felt a little of what my mother must have, all those years before.

Tonight, the bats end their show as they always do, disappearing into nowhere and nothing, one moment here and the next just gone, little magicians of the forest, and somehow I'm still not hungry. My friends have finished their cooking and are laughing around a fire, sharing a meal, but I'm not ready. Tonight, I feel like disappearing into the woods, wandering around in the starlight and reliving a life of walking through bats. I feel like thinking about my mother hiking through the woods in the dark. I feel like chatting with the bats.

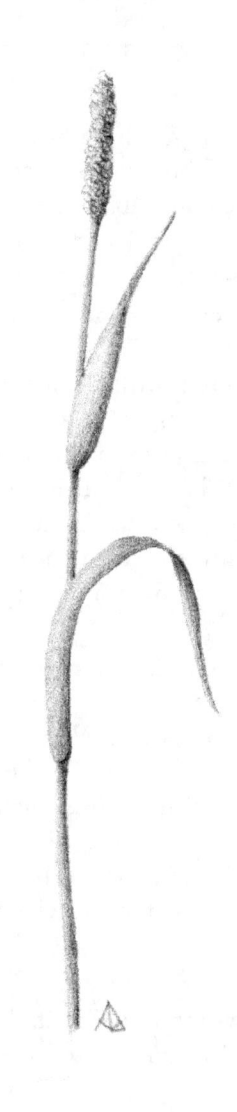

HOW TO BE ALONE

One of the first things I have to do when we come up to the mountain is to relearn how to be alone. For Annie, it's less difficult, I think. She's comfortably alone, and she works out of the house. She's by herself most of the time and knows how to be there. Besides, she's an introvert.

I am, however, an extrovert, and during the semester, I am surrounded by students and colleagues. I like to be with people and to hear them and to talk with them about everything. They give me energy. As the semester builds and my stress level grows, people give me insulation from the self-doubt that I live with. I am a born worrier and over-thinker. I feel guilt for things I have done even when they were the right thing to do. By the end of the semester, I find myself seeking people so I don't have to think about those things that are bothering me. They are distraction, and I need it.

I, like so many people, have a number of addictions. The most powerful of these is the distraction I get from being around other people. I feed this constantly. When I am not with students, I seek out my colleagues. I am on Facebook constantly, and I get a little high every time someone likes my post or comments on it. I have three email addresses for three different groups of people. It's not healthy to always be alone, but it is equally unhealthy to search for a group of people to help dispel the alienation and boost my endorphins.

I am not alone in this. The world, as Wordsworth put it, is too much with us. He wrote this line in 1802, and it hasn't gotten better, and my mind magnifies and creates problems, so soon I am thinking about all of the ways the world has failed me, or I have failed it.

The first part in learning to be alone is trying to go cold turkey. Connection to people is my drug. Silence is sobriety. We generally leave during the night to avoid traffic. Annie usually sleeps, and I try to turn off the radio. My drug is talking to people, and I do it to distract myself from painful thoughts, so I sit in silence for as long as I can take it as my mind goes over every slight and every failure, real and imagined, in my life. I sink lower and lower into an evil depression until I can't take it any longer. Usually, this lasts about two hours. That's when I turn on the radio or put on an audiobook to distract myself.

It's like this for days as I am setting up camp and getting ready for the next weeks or months in the mountains. Annie is there, and she's happy to talk to me. It's good to talk to her, but I can't yammer on constantly. Anyway, I'm trying to cure myself.

The key is not to distract myself. The key is not to be frightened of those thoughts. After a while they're not crowding in on me all at once. It's not a hurricane in my mind where I flit from one negative thought to the next. When that happens, I let my misgivings come, and I think my way through each one. Once I have thought about it and decided whether I can do anything about it, I can let it go.

This is the hardest part of the summer and the most difficult part of learning to be comfortably alone. If you are like me, and the world is too much with you, and you rely on social media and conversations to get through your day, this will be the hardest part for you as well. I find that it lasts a torturous three days. By the time that is done, I can do the real work of finding my own place in this world.

Learning how to be alone is both the most difficult and most important thing that we are doing. It forces a retraining of my brain. At the beginning of the semester, what I am doing is trying to help my students and my colleagues as much as possible. By the end of the semester, I am addicted to the stress. I both hate it and need it, and I am often looking for problems where they don't exist simply because that is what I have been doing, and it is the only thing that I have been doing, for the past months. Eventually, I cannot see the world except through the lens of my frustrations.

It is not necessary to go into the forest to find what I am truly looking for. I could do this on the ocean, in the desert, or even in the city. It's easier for me to find that thing in the forest because away from the Internet and my responsibilities I can see my addiction to stress for what it is. It's also easier to see what is truly meaningful and what simply does not matter.

I go into the forest, therefore, not to find what is outside in the world, but to discover what is inside of me.

THE CATKINS BURST ON THEIR OWN

Annie and I stand on the edge of Cahoon Meadow just a few miles into the backcountry talking about catkins, the way they explode into a kind of green fog of pollen around a pine tree when they reach the right temperature. The tree gets fuzzy for a moment and then the powder reshapes itself to fit wind currents.

I nod to the cloud. "I must be slowing down or something," I say to Annie. "This is the first year I've ever noticed that."

"Nah," she says. "This is just the first time you've lived like this."

She's right. It's been five weeks that we've been off grid and living in a tent. I've started to see the place in a way that I never would have before. Even when we stayed in a cabin, I would have been thinking about the emails that I need to send out or something I'd seen on television. Instead, I sit here watching nature's summer and working my way out of thought.

In a while, we start down the path. It's been a long hike today, but not a hard one. We woke before the sun, and it's still early. I don't know what time it is, and I don't care. To get down off this part of the mountain, we have to go down a long flight of stairs that someone carved into the rocks maybe fifty or a hundred years ago, and on our way, we meet a couple who look college-age coming up.

We step out of the way to let them pass, but they pause where they are, panting from the climb. The woman, out of breath, groans. The man laughs, "Don't worry about her," he says. "She's just not used to walking this far without capturing a Pokémon."

It seems like a snippy kind of comment, and I'm expecting some kind of fight to break out, but she leans on her walking stick and laughs. "He's not wrong, you know. I don't suppose you can catch a signal up there." She nods the way Annie and I have come.

I turn to Annie, but she just shrugs. "I'm sorry," I say, "But I don't know what you're talking about."

She explains it to me. Apparently, in the last five weeks, the cyber world has figured out a way to force people to leave their houses, chasing after Pokémon with cell phones. It's a global phenomenon the man tells me. Everyone in the world is doing it. Even his mother is doing it, and he names her age, which is younger than mine.

The young woman explains the game, and it sounds like a lot of fun. If I had a cell phone, which I don't, and lived within a signal, which I also don't, I would certainly be joining in. It's a rare time in our modern world when everyone is joining in on an experience and finding a shared joy. I try to remember another similar instance and can really only come up with the moon landing.

Everyone in the world is playing this game, I think, except Annie and me. We are certainly missing out. There is value in joining in with that kind of global phenomenon, but there is value to missing it as well.

We sit down on these stairs to catch up on so much that we have missed. People have been killed in France while celebrating Bastille Day. Gay men have been murdered in a nightclub by a homophobic psychopath. Black men have been killed in their cars with no provocation, and police officers have been ambushed in a flimsy excuse for retribution for those killings. The election goes on, they tell us, and the Olympics are coming up too, Zika virus or not.

Eventually, we all decide to push off. They have miles to go into their world of natural isolation, and I wish I were off with them. We're coming back to our base camp, which bumps into the other world every once in a while. "It's enough to make you forget about the catkins," I say.

"Nah," Annie says. "This isn't anything new."

She's right. It's chaos off the mountain, but when is it not? The giant pine trees that we've been watching this afternoon are old enough to have lived through World War II, Andrew Jackson, and Napoleon's hundred days. They've seen the moon landing too, and all of the modern Olympics. Nations come and go. Peace has been created and destroyed, but in that time, the temperature has gotten to be just warm enough every summer that the catkins have exploded their pollen into Cahoon Meadow. Sometimes people have seen it and sometimes not, but this year, we are here.

In a couple of months, I might be chasing Pokémon through the streets of Los Angeles, and I certainly will be voting, but at this moment, all I am is here.

GHOST OWL

I have always loved it here in the High Sierra at night, and it is magic this evening, when the owl drops out of its branch and floats above camp, going after a rodent I suppose, but there's something so unearthly about the way it moves through the sky that it seems more metaphor than living animal, or so are the thoughts I have when sitting alone in the dark next to a fire that's almost out watching the stars.

I supposed I have seen owls flap their wings, but I can't remember it. Mostly what I remember are nights like these when they have come out of nowhere and disappeared in a moment. I have never been with anyone when this happens, never been able to poke someone and point and talk about what we both have seen. In this, for me, they are like ghosts. They're so odd, so beautiful that I don't know if what I have seen is real, and there is no way for me to confirm that what I just witnessed wasn't a part of my imagination.

Tonight, I look up from my chair in this camp I have returned to for forty years now to see the face of a teenage boy hanging in the darkness, watching me. He's too skinny and wears a black Member's Only knock-off jacket. He tilts his head and watches me, silent and trying to figure me out.

I say, "John," and he's gone.

This, I understand, is the ghost of me, fourteen years old. He has slipped out of the cabin after everyone else went to sleep. Tonight, he's seen his first owl, and he thinks there's something magic about sneaking out and seeing that, like maybe he's cheated the world, like maybe this signifies that he's special somehow, destined to see things and know things that others can't.

I don't know about all of that, but I know that he's right on one count. Seeing that owl was magic.

I want to speak to him, and I remember where he went after he saw the great bird, so I douse the campfire and move toward the meadow where I spent so many of my childhood nights. There's a spot where I could sit on a rock and stare out across the grasses and just lose myself in not thinking.

I trudge my way through the night, no longer moving silently the way I would back in those days. Now my feet are heavy. They kick up dust behind me.

That kid up ahead of me, hiding from me, the ghost of the boy I used to be, doesn't trust adults, I know. He won't trust me now. He trusts things that don't lie to him. He trusts birds and rain. He trusts the earth and the thoughts buried deep in his head.

This year will be a year of owls for him. He'll be walking through the desert in late fall when he must come close to a nest and an owl buzzes him again and again. He will spend a night in a quarter mile square deep in the High Sierra listening to an owl call and trying to find it in the dark. He will be sure he saw one swooping over his Los Angeles neighborhood and not be able to convince anyone that he did.

I want to let him know that I believe him.

He's there at the meadow, alert to me and my heavy steps. He watches me from the rock, and I stop as I would stop so as not to spook a wary animal. We stare at each other for a moment, and then I blink, and he is gone.

Who knows where he is now? He can move through the woods better than anyone I've ever known, and I'll never catch him. Anyway, I should let him be. He is lost in his dreams of owls, and that's not a bad place to take up residence. He will haunt these woods forever.

HITCHHIKING WITH THE DEVIL

That night, I wake up sweating. My nightmare had something to do with the devil. I can remember Satan holding my wrists and making me smack myself in the face. In a guttural voice, he kept saying, "Why are you hitting yourself" over and over. When I wake, I naturally think of Mr. M who taught sixth grade at the Catholic school I attended as a child. He would have loved this vision of the devil as a kind of supernatural bullyboy, and no doubt could have told me of a saint who had actually lived the nightmare I described. Mr. M was our favorite teacher. When it came time for religion class, he would tell us tales of the weird and paranormal and then somehow bring that back to a discussion of Christianity.

In my half-sleep, I remember the story he told us about a young woman who was hitchhiking. She knew that it was the wrong thing to do, but she was foolish. She was picked up by a handsome man in an expensive car who drove her to the city. All the while, he told her about the life she could have, a life like his. All she had to do was make a lot of money. He had a dozen ways to get rich, and he started to tell them to her. None of them were legal, but they were foolproof. If she followed one of his many plans, she was sure to be rolling in money, clothes, and perfumes. She was drawn farther and farther into his world when she happened to drop something and glanced down. That was when she noticed that he had hooves instead of feet. She knew that he was the devil. At this moment, Mr. M lifted one finger and said, "Always remember that the devil can never hide his cloven hooves." Every single one of us in the room gasped.

I'm not sure exactly what the moral was here. There are some competing messages. It's something about not hitchhiking and not committing crimes for easy wealth. Also he seemed to be telling us that people in nice cars are bad, and good looking people are not to be trusted. Maybe he just wanted us to be aware of people's footwear.

I crawl out of my tent and wonder what those stories all those years ago had to do with religion and why he would bother to tell them. They were not a part of any kind of catechism I can imagine.

He told us about women who stopped being nuns and pledged themselves to Satan. They gained powers, but he wouldn't tell us what kind. He talked about young men who skipped church and smoked marijuana. He talked about children our age who gave false confessions as a kind of joke. I never understood how that was funny to those kids. It seemed kind of boring. What I did know was that the kids were going to go to hell. Almost all of his protagonists were doomed to burn unless they made abject and tearful confession pledging right then to become priests or nuns. In that case, they generally rose to glory as cardinals or mothers superior. He told us about saints who got into fist fights with the devil, and others who cast demons out of women everyone thought had been fornicators but were just possessed.

The fog rolled in as I was sleeping. Our camp is seven thousand feet high on the side of a mountain, and we must be very close to the top of the cloud because the moonlight is filtering through, lighting up the mist in brilliant white. For years after Mr. M's class, these woods would have been populated by satanic cult members, who would thrill at the idea that I might commit the smallest sin, thus starting down the path that would doom me. I would have thought of the devil trying to decide on a form for himself. It wasn't real fear but the kind you get from an amusement park or a horror movie. I could populate a forest with the boogey men of late night television.

For a moment, I wish Mr. M. could see this because I think this is what he was trying to get at. There is something of the ridiculous in who he was and what he was doing to us, but he had an incredibly difficult job that he thought was important. He was trying to convince a room full of eleven year olds that there are forces in this world much more powerful, much larger than a single person, and his names for these forces were God and Satan. The problem wasn't so much our age. It was that we were city kids who had never experienced the kinds of things that I am tonight.

At seven thousand feet, I am at the top of a bank of clouds and most of the forest and mountains too. There's just enough cloud here to make it glow, but I know there is likely a world of rain below me and some of the rain is seeping into the mountain and into caves that no one will ever see, and that animals no one has ever or will ever hear of live in their own biospheres cut off from the rest of the world. They are places of eternal mystery. Some of the rain falling tonight will feed those strange creatures, and in a hundred years or more, the rain will find its way back out of the mountain into our world, and people who have not been born yet will use it to feed themselves too.

If the students of Mr. M's sixth grade class had been allowed to experience my world tonight, to live in direct contact with the earth rather than be separated from it, his job, at least half of it, would have been easy. He would not have had to convince those kids that there were forces in this world that were larger than they were. My guess is that in an hour or so, the wind is going to kick up and drive the clouds up high, and I will be fully engaged in the rainstorm. Maybe the lightning will rage around me. I'll watch from my tent as the animals shelter, and the trees will bend back and forth in the wind.

In a world like that, it becomes quickly apparent how small each of us is and how powerful everything else is, so he'd have half his job done. Now, he'd only have to convince us that these powers were controlled by God. Maybe that part wouldn't have been hard either. In any case, he wouldn't have had to come up with his stories of redeemed sinners who became saints, fallen nuns doomed to hell, or children who foolishly hitchhiked with the devil.

GLACIERS

In this fourth year of the drought, what will turn out to be the last year of the drought, someone tells me that most of the ancient glaciers have melted in the High Sierra. I don't know if that's true. I think about that as Wolverton Creek runs through our campground. These are the glaciers that Muir identified and named over a hundred years ago, glaciers that were ancient when he saw them first.

The ancient trees, the sequoias and foxtail pines, have never known a time when the glaciers were not there. They have been in these mountains before people were on this continent.

The idea of these glaciers and their loss stays with me all summer long. In June, I'm making tea, and I play a kind of morbid game with myself. I think that the snowfield Muir walked across is running down Wolverton Creek right then. I think the tea I'm making spilled off his beard and into the glacier below.

In July, I imagine that the water flowing past me fell when Boudica had her doomed uprising just as I am lighting the fire for the night. I imagine that it is flowing past me at the rate of a year every five minutes, which is as good a guess as I am bound to have. Later that month, I figure that the water has shifted into a prehistory before no one could write. At that time, mammoths still wandered California. They're gone too, and for that matter the grizzly bears we still have on our flag.

By late August, I suppose that they're all gone. It's an exaggeration, but as I'm wandering through a predawn hike, I figure it's over. All these years, and it's gone.

The next months bring snow and rain. We have the wettest year in recent memory, and I imagine the glaciers being filled up. Or maybe these are new ones being created. They are back though. The clouds snow hard and unsentimentally. Down in the valley at night, I listen to the rain in bed. I am awakened by it. All of those years, and that living was released into the air, and maybe this year's snow will lie buried under more years' accumulation.

I decide in the drowsiness that comes at a two a.m. wake up that I will be the first one to climb to the high country and walk across the infant snowfields. I want them to be imprinted with the memory of my shoe. I want the glaciers to think of me forever as their firstborn. I want them to be proud. I want them to know my name.

QUAIL

I am lost in an early summer hike daydream up near Little Baldy. This has been a year of water, and the animal populations have exploded. The forest is filled with bears and deer. One mother left her fawn with us for three days.

I can't hear very well, and I don't think I would have heard the quail call even if I could because I am lost in a daydream about Muir, how he wandered these forests with his eyes open and with a scientific knowledge of these plants and rocks. In my sleepwalk, I step into the middle of a quail family, mother, father, and perhaps ten hatchlings, who scatter because of me to either side of the trail. Mother and father go left and so do about half the chicks. The other half go right and begin to call frantically to their parents who call back to them to come. I take two steps back and sit down, not wanting to terrorize them anymore.

I try to imagine what John Muir would say or do. I talk to him, speak to the air asking for his guidance the way some of my Irish ancestors might have spoken to St. Teresa. For all I do, I cannot summon him or his help. The dead are often silent here, and they don't ever seem to come on request.

That leaves me a half hour to sit here then and think about the nature of life and death and the forest. It leaves me the chance to slow down again and focus on the present moment, and I am glad Muir is wandering his personal forests, that he left me alone. I would thank him if I could. I would shake his hand and talk about quail.

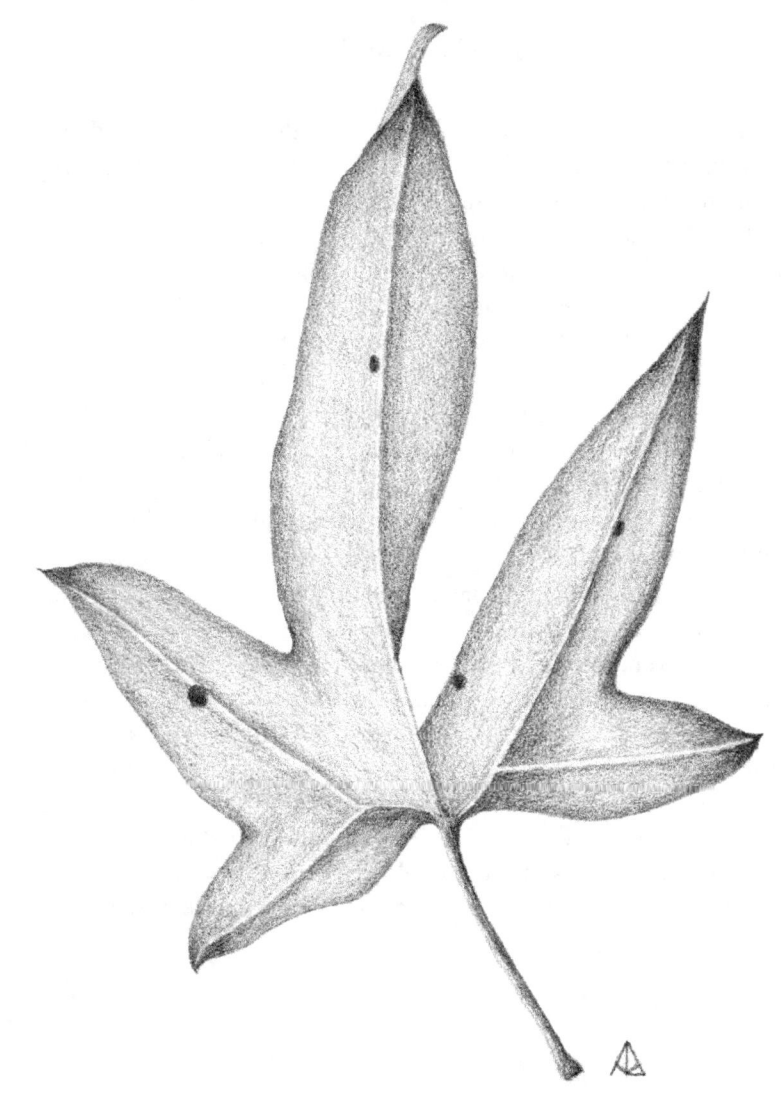

SOOTY GROUSE

Up near Alta Peak, I come upon a male sooty grouse. He is standing on the edge of the cliff looking down into the hundred foot chasm below him calling in a throaty voice. I am not a birder although I have always admired them, so I don't know what exactly his call means. Perhaps he is calling for his mate who has gone down into the canyon. Do they fly? I don't know. Maybe he has just lost the love of his life. She has died, and he is calling after her. Maybe he is just trying to locate friends.

I am alone here on this mountain, the only person on this trail as far as I know, perhaps the only human for ten miles, and this is my afternoon. I look out with the grouse past the city of Three Rivers to the San Joaquin Valley, and he thinks about his family, and I think about my wife.

Finally, there is a call back from down below. He cocks his head, and it comes again. He's the size and roughly the shape of a small chicken, so I'm surprised when he bounces off the edge and flutters down. I watch him make his awkward way through the air into the valley floor, and realize that I am here to witness a kind of truth, but I'm not sure exactly what it is. I don't know how to articulate it, and there's no one to talk it over with, and anyway what would we say? In any case, part of the truth has to do with the fact that I am completely alone here, apart from all other humans and lost in the long thoughts possible only when I am.

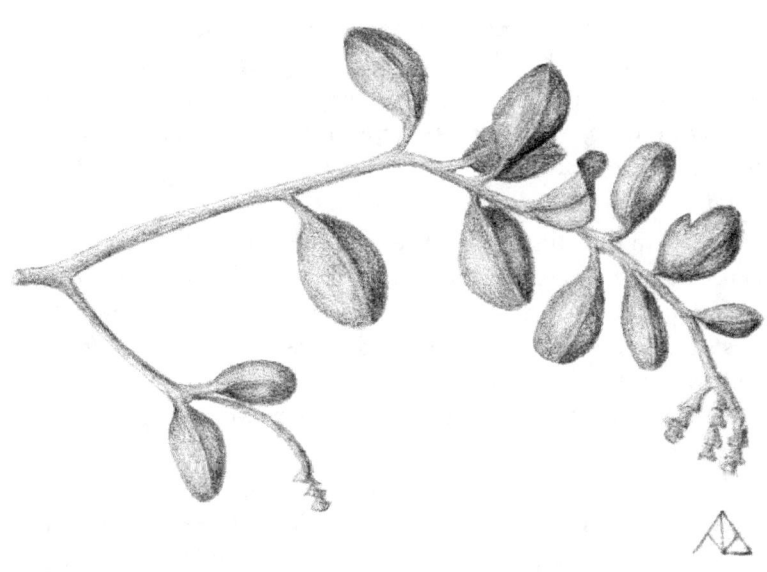

CONTROLLED BURN

At the beginning of the spring, the rangers do a controlled burn near Sunset Rock. The trail to Sunset Rock has always been one of my favorites. It's a gentle mile-long hike along the rim above the Kaweah River through oaks and pines. There is a little meadow that feels wetter than others to me for some reason. The grasses are always taller than my six feet.

We get into the mountains in the early summer, and the fire is nearly out. There is still a smoldering stump, but otherwise nothing burns. Anyway, there is nothing left to burn. Except for the mature trees, everything between the meadow and rock has been turned to black ash. It's a strange thing to see. It's a terrifying thing to see.

I grew up at a time when fire was equated with sin. During breaks between Saturday morning cartoons, Smokey the Bear would point directly at me and tell me that it was my fault that forests burned. After all, only I could prevent them, he would say. That was quite a responsibility. Some programs would go on to show woodlands that had burned, and they would suggest that those woods were just gone forever.

Here, in this weird otherworld of after-fire, that seems as if it is true, even though I know it is wrong. What I know is that the bushes might be gone, and the little trees too, but there are seeds working their way into the rich soil the sooty ash is creating. By the late summer, the burning smell is nearly gone, but my boots still kick up the ash when I walk through the area.

During the next spring in my breaks between classes, I dream of those places. A friend of mine is a ranger, and she told me that morel mushrooms come out in April or May when the ground is muddy with snow melt, and the air is still cold. Most people don't have vacation time to come up to see it, so the people who live there hunt them. She goes out with a camp stove, a pan, and some butter.

The mushrooms thrive best in places of recent fire. They like the nutrients in the ash, and they bloom in droves. I imagine her sitting there by herself, frying them up on her stove, in this place that is slowly turning back into the forests I know.

The forest is, of course, replanting itself. Out of the rich ash, there is a carpet of sapling pines mixed with wildflowers. The black ash is still visible, but it also makes all of the other colors pop that much more vibrantly.

By the time I'm back in the summer, I can still tell that a fire was through here, but the forest in this area is thriving. There is new life and it is filled with birds. The duff layer is gone, and the earth seems to have absorbed the powdery ash somehow. New views of the canyon have opened up as well and I can see a road below us and in some places the river. This trail that has long been one of my favorites has been renewed by the fire. It is the most spectacular spot in the forest.

AIR

When Scott and Carly get into camp, their car is covered with rain water. Camp is at seven thousand feet. Up here, everything is clear. It's sunny, at least.

It's impossible to say that where we are staying is clear. People expect the mountain air to be clean and pure. After all, there are very few cars here. It's difficult to imagine unless the fact is pointed out to you, that all ecosystems are connected. While some might have some distance and grow up independently, they are all interconnected because the earth is a single ecosystem. The fact is that much of the High Sierra is heavily polluted. San Francisco typically has relatively nice, fresh air. The air is nice because the ocean breezes push its smog out to the valley where it gets trapped in the Western Sierra. There is Fresno, Sacramento, Bakersfield, a host of smaller cities and farms that use pesticides. The mountain air is the same as the valley air, which is to say, not good.

I am looking up into the gray sky and thinking about this and thinking about Scott and Carly's car. "Where did you hit rain?" I ask.

"Just like two miles from here," Scott says. "It's flooded down the road."

These are, of course, mountain roads, so two miles is also a thousand feet lower than we are. Now that I think about it, I have been hearing booms in the distance. As someone who normally lives with a view of the Ontario Airport, I am used to tuning out sounds. I realize that the booms I have been tuning out has been thunder, the whole world below me in thunderstorm, but I live too high in the air for that.

Scott and Carly are here to help us talk to the students about the things that live in the air. Carly is anyway. Scott is a poetry professor and writer, and he'll talk to my students. Carly is a scientist who specializes in squirrels. She's going to talk about these little rodents who live in a kind of middle world that we don't see so often. Of course, many of them come down to the ground to feast on acorns or seeds, but much of their lives is in the middle world between the canopy of the treetops and the ground we live in.

My favorite is the chickaree, a little squirrel that climbs up the trunks of the giant sequoias and chews through the stems of the cones. They can do this at a rate of one cone a second. Years ago, I heard thud, thud, thud and came through the woods looking for what was making this strange sound only to find a monarch losing its cones. No one is sure what compels them to their quest, but without it, the forest might not repopulate with the giant trees. It is one of the mysteries that lies within the woods.

"It's chaos down there," Carly says, but her eyes are shining. She is like me, or maybe like I used to be when I had more vitality. Her love for the woods and those things that live halfway up in the sky keeps her moving. It keeps her thinking. It is an endless set of questions and mysteries. She moves through the woods at a pace only she seems to be able to keep. When something ahead is really interesting, she'll start jogging and then running, and I'm not sure that she realizes she's doing it, so caught up in the fascination of the woods.

Scott is like Annie. He loves these places too, but he is not so wrapped up that he loses himself to it. I think more important to Scott is that he loves Carly, and he likes to see her so blissful that she forgets where she is.

In any case, we spend the day looking up toward the sky. During the afternoon it is to see the little mammals that live there. She talks about the sequoia beetle too, that like the chick-aree helps to repopulate the sequoias. It eats the flesh of the cones freeing the seeds. If we're lucky, we'll get to see one of these beetles, but I don't think so. They live in the air after all, and rarely come down.

As the day moves into night, we watch the bats above us, and I ask her what the chances of seeing flying squirrels is. They live up here too, but I'm not sure if I've ever seen one. Neither, it turns out, has she. They're nocturnal and shy, but she tells us where to look and what to look for. We turn our attention for one night away from the fire and watch dark treetops framed in dark gray skies. We don't see any of the squirrels that live there tonight, but there are stars, planets, the moon, airplanes, and satellites flying by.

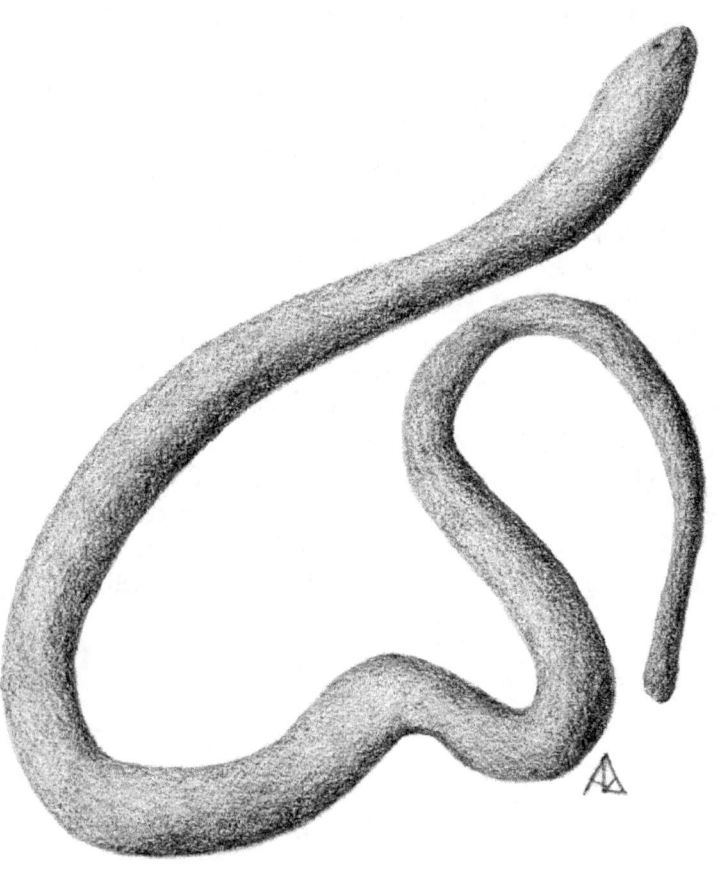

Rubber Boa

I move out of the circle of firelight where Annie and my students are sitting, talking about the day. I'm carrying the leftover food down to the bear box. On my way back up, I have my flashlight pointed down so I don't trip when a flesh-colored flash catches my eye to the left. I shine my beam in the direction and find a rubber boa squirming through the powdery dirt of the road making its way to the safety of the grass next to camp. I could call to my friends around the campfire, but they would not get here before he hid. I flip off the flashlight and let him move on in peace.

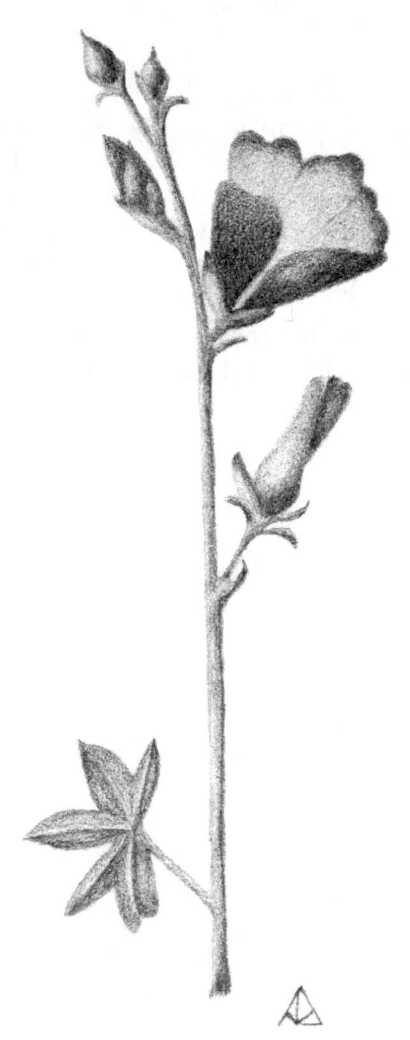

HAZELWOOD MEADOW

On my hike into class, I drop down into Hazelwood Meadow. It's a warm morning, maybe seventy-five degrees, and the sun is out. A breeze is swaying the tops of the trees, and I stop a moment to feel it riffling my clothes.

As I stand there, the outer edge of a cloud pushes its way through the pine trees and down the hill into this bowl of meadow where I am standing. In one moment, perhaps thirty seconds, the fog swirls into the forest over me and around me, and the temperature drops to chilling, and my world is transformed from bright summer to early fall.

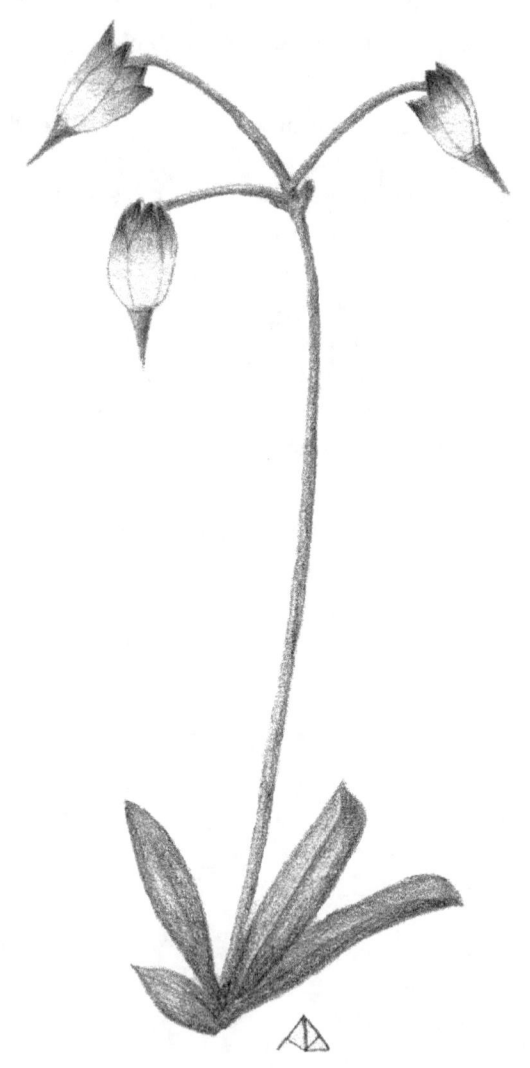

How to Live without Electric Lights

This isn't complicated. Our eyes aren't built for flashlights. They were never meant to use them. When the sun goes down, if we aren't surrounded by artificial lights, our eyes adjust to the moon and starlight.

On those nights when everyone goes to bed, and I'm still not tired, I go for long walks in the forest without a flashlight. I stay on paths or roads, of course, and I stay out of the areas where the forest is dense. If you don't blind yourself with the equipment of the modern day, walking through the forest in the middle of night is easy.

These moments I have in the forest at night are my own. Almost no one else is up and out, and those who are, are confined to the little pools of light that they carry with them. To those people, the night is terrifying because they can't see beyond that tiny pool of light. Typically, I'll walk to the meadow and stare out across the grasses. Sometimes I'll stand there for hours of joyous meditation. But I have climbed to the top of Moro Rock and looked across the San Joaquin Valley and up on the ridge line to look across the tops of the Giant Sequoia groves. I have contemplated satellites and meteor showers.

It isn't the dark that makes the night terrifying. It is the wrong kind of light. That light defines our life and gives us a false sense of borders. That light says that here our worlds have a kind of safety but beyond that, twenty feet away from us, is a world of chaos. That light is a lie that we keep telling ourselves. Beyond it, is just the world, less chaotic to my mind than the world lit up in a pantomime of the day.

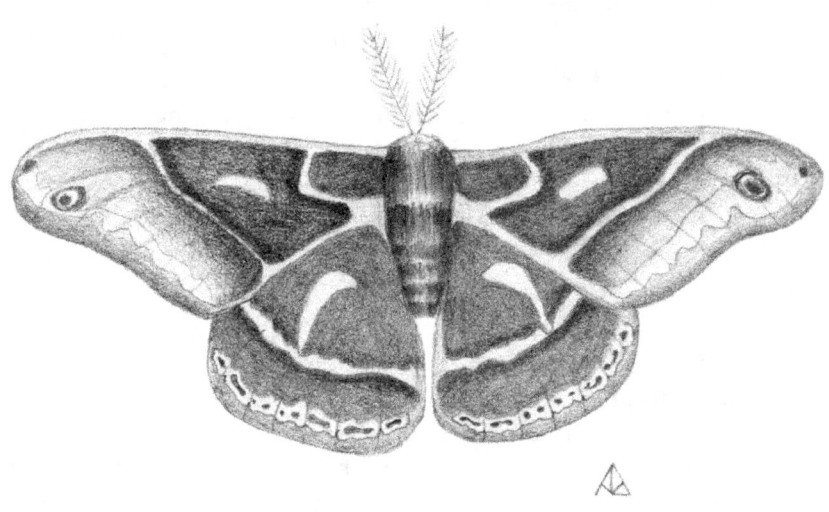

Midnight in Wolverton Meadow

On the last night in the High Sierra for the summer, I sit with my students and my wife, and we talk about the last week. It's been a good week. They all have been. We toast each other and I think about what tomorrow will be like. I am not afraid of it, and I do not hate the city. I am ready for the coming semester. It will be at times frustrating, and at the same time beautiful. I like watching people grow into the intellectuals they can be, after all.

One by one people go into their tents, and I stay up until the last one says good night. One of my jobs is to douse the fire. I don't trust anyone else to do it. I tried once, and I kept waking up to look out to see if the world was on fire.

When the fire circle is cold, floating in four buckets of water and muddy, I stand for a while, leaning against a tree, waiting for my eyes to adjust to the dark. It doesn't take long. The night isn't very dark. With no headlights or streetlights to ruin my night vision, soon even this moonless night is bright, and I go for a walk without a flashlight down the road. The stars brighten the world differently than the sun does. Everything in this wood stands out distinctly at night and apart from everything else. A boulder, a tree, a stick. The animals are all asleep or at least silent, so the only sound is the wind and my footsteps.

I come up to the overlook where I can see the meadow, and I watch it turn silver in the night. The cool wind is on my face, and it riffles the grasses. I have forgotten now that I will be in the city tomorrow. I have forgotten my students, my place in this world, my wife, and even myself. I have left behind my worry about the campfire. Right now is all that matters.

ABOUT THE AUTHORS

Ann and John Brantingham met in London on a joint study abroad program through Mt. San Antonio College and Rio Hondo College and fell just about immediately in love. They were drawn together by a joint passion for art, literature, the forest, the city, dogs, and each other. They've tried to live their lives compassionately, and they believe that compassion is their highest purpose and most noble aspiration. They came closer to their own humanity in Sequoia and Kings Canyon National Parks where they volunteered and lived for nine summers in a van. The time they've shared with the volunteers, employees, and friends up in the parks means more to them than they can say. What they hope more than anything is that you disappear into your own natural haven and find out a little more about yourself. They keep discovering who they are again and again.

PHOTO BY ALEXIS RHONE FANCHER

112 N. Harvard Ave. #65
Claremont, CA 91711

chapbooks@bamboodartpress.com
www.bamboodartpress.com